An Anthology
OF POEMS
By Anthony Warren Bardsley

An Anthology OF POEMS
By Anthony Warren Bardsley

Copyright © 2015 by Anthony Bardsley.

ISBN: Softcover   978-1-4990-9028-4
              eBook   978-1-4990-9029-1

All rights reserved. No part of this book may be reproduced or transmitted in any form or by any means, electronic or mechanical, including photocopying, recording, or by any information storage and retrieval system, without permission in writing from the copyright owner.

Any people depicted in stock imagery provided by Thinkstock are models, and such images are being used for illustrative purposes only.
Certain stock imagery © Thinkstock.

This book was printed in the United States of America.

Rev. date: 01/15/2015

To order additional copies of this book, contact:
Xlibris
0-800-056-3182
www.xlibrispublishing.co.uk
Orders@xlibrispublishing.co.uk
669473

CONTENTS

Chapter 1   Through The Good Times 9
Chapter 2   Paradise 10
Chapter 3   I Walked 11
Chapter 4   My Friend 12
Chapter 5   The Romiley Trek 13
Chapter 6   I Used To Get Up 14
Chapter 7   Summer 15
Chapter 8   Nature 16
Chapter 9   Tablets And Pills 17
Chapter 10   Mother 18
Chapter 11   The Worker 19
Chapter 12   Summer Heart 20
Chapter 13   Romiley Arms 21
Chapter 14   Manchester Lad 22
Chapter 15   Soldiers 23
Chapter 16   I Feel So Happy Today 24
Chapter 17   It's Christmas 25
Chapter 18   The Good Times 26
Chapter 19   The Idiot 27
Chapter 20   In The Mental Home 28
Chapter 21   Pain 29
Chapter 22   Young Girl 30
Chapter 23   My Lovely Amphetimine Girl 31
Chapter 24   Peace 32
Chapter 25   The Sunset 33
Chapter 26   Over The Hills 34
Chapter 27   To Sail A Ship Far Away 35
Chapter 28   Gerard 36
Chapter 29   My Best 37
Chapter 30   Stare 38
Chapter 31   Curtains 39
Chapter 32   Leaking Pipes 40
Chapter 33   Radiators Old 41

Chapter 34	The Rain	42
Chapter 35	The Beautiful Butterfly	43
Chapter 36	2001	44
Chapter 37	The Snob	45
Chapter 38	A Walk Through Stockport	47
Chapter 39	Tramps Not Thieves	48
Chapter 40	Mum And Dad And Me	49
Chapter 41	Worldly Goods	51
Chapter 42	Stuck In My Room	52
Chapter 43	Alley Road	53
Chapter 44	Up Romiley	55
Chapter 45	Sweet Child Of Mine	56
Chapter 46	Old People	57
Chapter 47	Hospital Bed	58
Chapter 48	Stay-At-Home Bill	60
Chapter 49	A Child's View Of Jesus	61
Chapter 50	I'll Be Ready	62
Chapter 51	The Cold's Coming	63
Chapter 52	The Grey White Dove	64
Chapter 53	The White Dove	65
Chapter 54	The Losing Card	66
Chapter 55	O Young Destination	67
Chapter 56	All The Fun Of The Fair	68
Chapter 57	The Green Grass	69
Chapter 58	Hatred	70
Chapter 59	Staring Through My Room	71
Chapter 60	The Queen Bee	72
Chapter 61	Winter Chills	73
Chapter 62	Summer Brings Lightning	74
Chapter 63	Sunlight	75
Chapter 64	Earth And Stars	77
Chapter 65	Having Not And Have Nothings	78
Chapter 66	I Saw A Shooting Star	79
Chapter 67	I Saw That Plane	80
Chapter 68	In The Care Home	81
Chapter 69	Little Childhood Joe	83
Chapter 70	My Mother Cared For Me	85
Chapter 71	The Mountain Of Heaven	87
Chapter 72	Anthony's Quotations	89

ANTHONY'S STORY

Anthony Warren Bardsley was born on October 14th 1960 to Warren and Joan Bardsley of 18 Riversdale View Woodley Stockport. Anthony used to have five sisters and two brothers. His sister Florence died in 2002 aged 45. In the following Anthology you will find a poem dedicated to Florence.

Anthony's life has not been easy in his late teens he was diagnosed with the mental illness Schizophrenia and more recently Epilepsy. Despite his disability Anthony has for years produced a rich vein of poetry which we hope you will enjoy in this booklet. His great grandfather known as "Thade Gowran" or Timothy McGovern was a writer of poems and ballads in his native Abbeyfeale, County Limerick, Republic of Ireland. Anthony has inherited Thades great gift. He has great insight and a compassion for his fellow men and women. One of Anthony's great sayings is "Perfection is a weakness"

We hope that Anthony's poems may be as perfect as possible for you, and you will get a flavour of this poets great talent from the village of Romiley Cheshire.

THROUGH THE GOOD TIMES

through the good times and the bad
the happy and the sad
carry on, carry on

the sadness and the fears
the heartache and the tears
carry on, carry on

the remembrance and the years
the loneliness and the fears
carry on, carry on

your darkness and tears
carry on, carry on

in the end you will win
so take it on the chin
your prize you will realize
in the heavens in the sky
you'll finally go home
and never be alone
just shine on, just shine on

PARADISE

Rich men found their goals.
Poor people find their souls.
Heaven lies in their screams.
City of gold in the city of dreams.

Through the money of screams,
Paradise! Paradise!
In the city of goals.

For one future we hold,
Things got tried in the hall of fate.
Paradise! Paradise! It's too late.

Plenty in time lives in a made paradise.
Make paradise the dream.
Peace in a power to paradise.

By Anthony Warren Bardsley

August 2008.

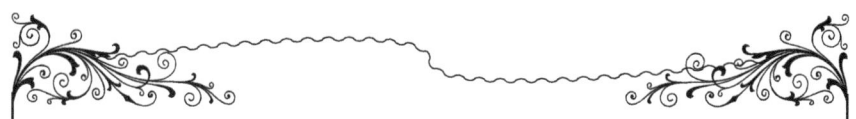

I WALKED

I walked down the ice,
It was nice.
I walked down the street,
it was neat.

In the sun ray of the snow,
Far through the snow.
In the windmill,
In the heat.

Down the road with a heavy load.
Up the stairs in the kitchen,
In the lift down the veranda.
Down the stream, in the city.

What a pity in the city.
The windy city, the city was dirty rather smirky.
Up in the sky, home and dry.
In the head so fly.

MY FRIEND

You are my friend right to the end.
I remember you right to the end.

With a smile you're my friend right to the end.
You taught me how to give.
I remember you my friend right to the end.

Now you are gone,
I can't carry on.

I remember you my friend right to the end.

By Anthony Warren Bardsley

August 2008.

THE ROMILEY TREK
By Anthony Warren Bardsley

I went for a walk around Romiley
I saw the lovely trees
I went past the Romiley Forum
I went through the park
On the swings and roundabout.
I went on the slide
I played football, I bought some lemonade and some sweets
and a packet of crisps.
It was a lovely day,
It was very warm and sunny.
The park was green, the trees were brown.
The wooden bench was brown.
The birds were flying in the sky.
The dogs were barking.
It was a lovely day in the park.
The rain had fallen overnight
and the sparrows were splashing around.
The water was transparent
It was lovely and fresh
Fresh enough to drink.
The birds were sipping the water,
The worms were bobbing out,
The ants were crawling,
The snails were sliding.
I like Romiley, there are lots of hills and lovely scenery.

Werneth Low is very high up,

There are Kestrels there, Swallows and Swifts.

The grass is green,

The hills are pleasant.

Werneth Low is the start of the Pennines.

I like the blue sky.

I USED TO GET UP

I used to get up when the sun came up
I played football on the Marple Park
I played until it went dark

I came home along the canal
I walked through the tunnel
Onto fields where cattle fed
On the seed of grass

I saw some frogs along the path
me and my mates ran with a rush
I suddenly slipped and I nearly fell in
my mates thought I was daft
We went through the mud and damp
walking a long way back to home
Made home with the best of lads
making home to the camp

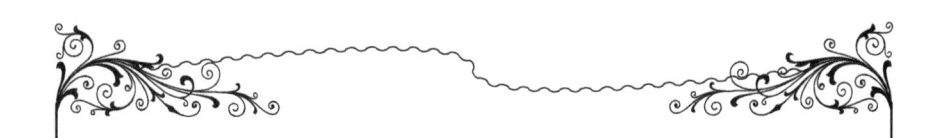

SUMMER

I remember the summer
The sunshine glistens on the mountain top
The waterfall fell on to the torrent river

And all the land began to quiver
The cold wind it made me shiver
I felt alone, in such a dither

The sun's rays shone on the soft stoney ground
I felt alone, around the swallow sang in the air
The sunshine shines all over the village square
And the moon shone in the midnight air

NATURE

The Swallows flying in the air.

Sparrows dipping their beak in the puddles in the ground.
Snails walking gracefully through the
ground making a very slow sound.

Doves flying in the air.
Animals hibernating without a care.

Bats flying in the air, hunting worms in the ground.

Shrubs growing all along the path.
Gardeners having their last laugh.

Through their share, birds in the air eating their share.

Tramps in the city dirtying their care.
Nature is cruel so just beware.

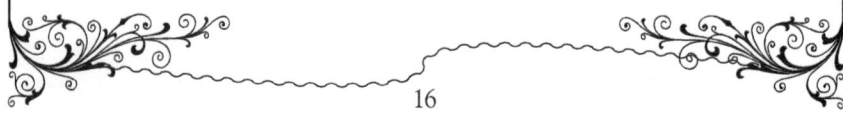

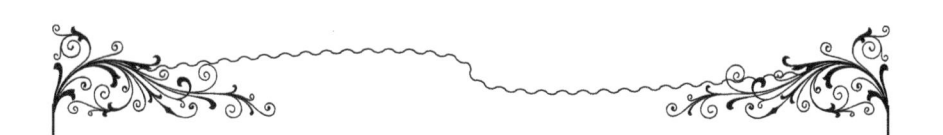

TABLETS AND PILLS

So many times I feel my ills, I grab my tablet and pills.
The cold snow and winter chills I grasp my pills.
Crazy through the day I grasp my pills.
Sometimes distorted hills.
I grasp my pills.
Summer days I grasp my pills.
I live my life I grasp my pills.
So when I die I won't grasp my tablet and pills.

By ANTHONY WARREN BARDSLEY

MOTHER

I remember my Mother I would not ask for another,
A Mother so dear so nice and sincere,
A gem from the isle, you had a lovely smile,
Dressed in Satin and Lace you had a certain style.
A mother true and true no one could hate you.
You taught me to love a gift from above.
You never gave in you took it on the chin.

I will always remember a mother like you.
I will see you again on my final breath.
In heaven with a smile.

THE WORKER

The worker tends the land.

He sows the seed, he wets the sand.

He clears the path.

He mows the grass.

He digs the field he yields the grass.

The worker works from morn till night. Starlight, sun bright.
The gardener digs the soil, from night till dawn they toil.
He sweats till noon at the sundune.
In the middle of June, he harvests till noon.

Tonight he harvests!

(Anthony says he wrote this poem in honour
of his Father, Warren Paul Bardsley).

SUMMER HEART

Summer heart in sundew rays.

Rainbows, clouds and rainy days.

Summer flowers, and daily care wares.

Decayed flowers and cotton wares.

Business men counting their shares.

Daily amaze their wares.

ROMILEY ARMS

I took a walk around Romiley Arms,
walking down Chadkirk Farms.

Fat bellied men drinking whiskey and beer,
chasing away their sufferings.

Landlady serving behind the bar, serving whiskey and neat.
Watching the traffic clear.

Children in the school, dancing in the garden.
Walking with a slogan on their cardigans.

By Anthony Warren Bardsley
(March 2008)

MANCHESTER LAD

Manchester lad! You're not so bad.
A lovely lad.

Manchester, you're a different breed,
Walking down Manchester overspills.

Down Albert Square,
So cocky without a care.

Manchester Piccadilly and Victoria Station,
Straight down the street with a high imagination.

Making music with the local talent, café in the street,
New wave music in the chippy.

Walking down the street without a care.
You're such a good lad it's such a pity.
You're a pop star in the City,
Watching Manchester City.

By Anthony Warren Bardsley
(March 2008)

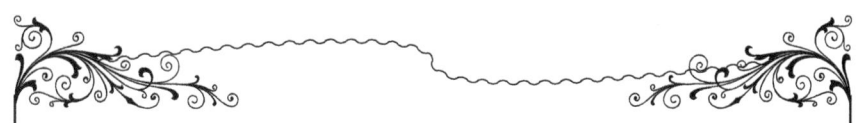

SOLDIERS

When fit men go to die, so what do they go to get their fill?
In a coffin in the ground from American Hill.

The men died for their will.
They battled against the desert sand.

They died in a desert town in the great desert night,
in a Babylonian garrison.

Go from the sand!
The soldiers were live meat in the desert sand.

I FEEL SO HAPPY TODAY

I feel so happy today
I think I might go out and play
The trees are green
The grass is fluorescent
The sky is blue
There is a lot to do

Things are going my way
I feel so happy today
It's a lovely day
I feel so happy today
The birds are singing
The church bells are ringing

It is a lovely day
I feel so gracious and proud
A lot is allowed
I feel so happy today
I think things might be going my way

The sun is burning
My happiness is returning
I feel so happy today
I think I might go out and play
My way it's a lovely day

I feel so happy today
I think I might go out and play

By Anthony Bardsley
October 2005

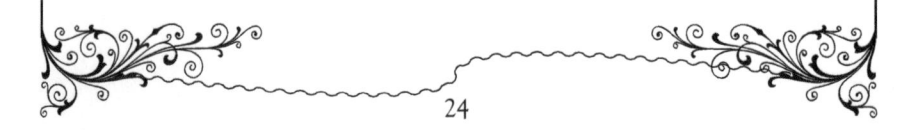

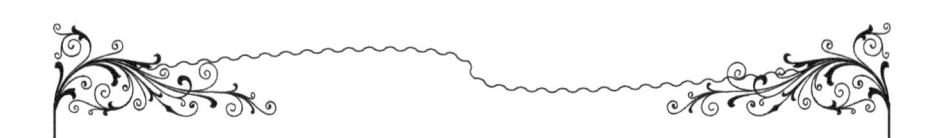

IT'S CHRISTMAS

It's Christmas so I chase the hills.
    Dismiss the winter chills.

Christmas relishes your ideals.

May you wipe away your blues.
Washing away your shoes.

Realizing your views.
Wipe away your blues.

Realize your choice.

It's Christmas, chase away your blues!

THE GOOD TIMES

I remember the good times, the windy view,
the morning dew, the jetful moon.
The sunset of June.

The rocky road, trouble once forgetting the bells.
Together we cross hands across the sands.

Finally find the view.
I remember the dew.
In heaven the sun,
Sooner or later seen heaven sent.

With you the world finally came through.

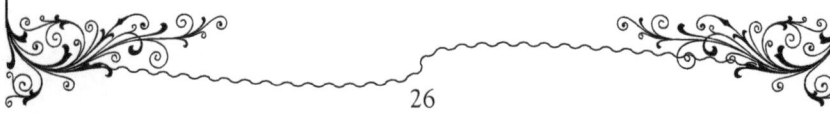

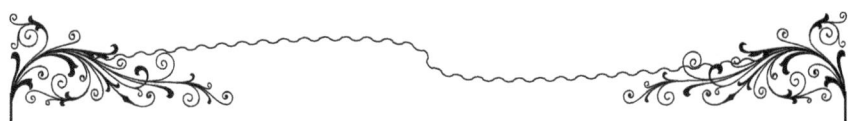

THE IDIOT

A wise old thing, happy mind.
A peaceful thing sleeps at night awake at light.
No mental fight.

He drinks tea and coffee and orange fruit.

From night till noon he never cries, a simple heart not so small.
They say pride before fall.

He's the cleverest of them all,
Although his mind is so small.

He hasn't got a brain, they say pride before fall.

He's the cleverest of them all, although his mind is so small.

By Anthony Warren Bardsley

IN THE MENTAL HOME

In the Mental Home I saw funny faces.
People doped on drugs, and different races.

Strangest people with mental cases.

White Collar workers helping the lame.
All the people so insane.

All have trouble with the pain.
Different troubles sunshine and rain.
Slowly walking down the ward, Doctors hand out their pills.

Straight Jacket cases, sitting on rugs, sitting on couches.
Drinking tea on footstools and dressing down ladies.
Night cases, all people crying with care.
Remember people in care, beware!

PAIN

Pain in my eyes,
Pain in my smile,
Pain in my style,
Pain in my heart.
Pain because I'm smart.

Pain in my face,
Pain in my soul,
Pain in my confidence,
Pain in my esteem.
Pain is not what it seems.

Pain in my laughter,
Pain in my fears,
Pain in my punishment,
Pain in my soul,
Pain in my triumphant,
Pain in my goal,
Pain in my stupidness,
Pain in my heart,
Pain from the start.
Pain because I'm small.

YOUNG GIRL

Young girl why do you fly?
You show the way to go home, you stay in the town,
With a long flowing dress, with a certain smile.

In the sunshine you have to go.
Lost and found, homeward bound,
Where your certain found.
Off the ground, homeward bound.
Without a sound on the ground.

MY LOVELY AMPHETIMINE GIRL

What a lovely girl, my lovely Amphetimine girl.
I wonder where you smile,
You have a certain style.
You have a certain smile.

What a Tophemine pill to cure your ill.
Start healing your soul of Amphetimine drink.
You do not know what to do my lovely Amphetimine girl.
You have a certain style my lovely Amphetimine girl.

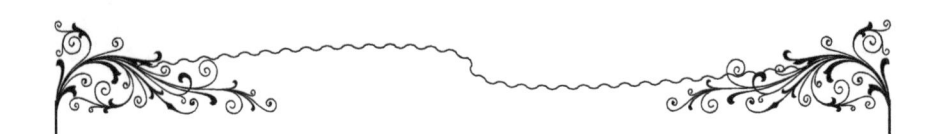

PEACE

Peace is sweet, peace is grand.
Peace is loving when we understand.
Peace is love, peace is good.
Peace is sweet, peace is loving.
In a family, peace is me, peace is you.
Peace is knowing what to do.
Peace is loving, peace is sharing.
Peace is loving, peace is caring.
Peace is wise, peace is knowledge.
Peace is loving yourself, peace is LOVING GOD.
Peace is Christ, peace is lord.
Peace comes from your mothers umbilical cord.
Peace is God, peace is best.
Peace is having a good nights rest.
Peace is free, peace is love.
Peace comes from heaven above.
But most of all peace is love.

THE SUNSET

The sunset shone over the dawn of June.

The tangerine sky illuminated in the light.

Start bright, start bright, for January old now.
I have a terrific goal to save my heart, to save my soul.

The distant sun, a better view.

In lament a sky blue not knowing what to do.

I am a man not knowing what to do.

Still coming through the fog,

Struggling through to find my point of view.

Still coming through.

OVER THE HILLS

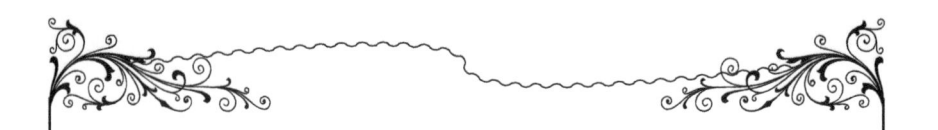

Over the hills down the stream,
Down the valley so green.
The sunshine over the river.
The fresh water made you shiver.
I walk on a long, over the land.
The seaside and the sand.
The sun shines so grand,
A distant view of the sea,
So lovely to me.
A land so free and familiar.
The ocean was so green,
So fluorescent and serene.
An ocean covered scene.
A land so soft and pleasant.
So green and caresses the land.
Life's a dream so fluorescent and "so green".

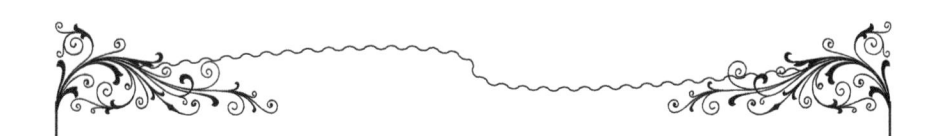

TO SAIL A SHIP FAR AWAY

Far away from the Winter's gloom.
From the sadness in my room,
far from the tears.
To sail a ship so far away.
In an Island in the sun,
From the darkness I did run.
A better land for me and you,
Away from the cold winters due.
A land to start anew,
With so much more to do.
A better life for me and you.
Faraway from a better view.

GERARD

Gerard is a sunny boy, brought his mum so much joy,

A kind hearted soul doing lots for his mother,

A good son and brother, my special brother.

MY BEST

Today I'm going to try my best,

I'll help everyone

I'll try some rest.

But it won't be like a test,

I'll finally find my zest.

STARE

I stare at the table,

When I am able

On the food and the plate,

It looks so great.

CURTAINS

The curtains cover the windows,

Like the darkness in my soul.

I only have one goal

And I've finally found my soul

LEAKING PIPES

The pipes are leaking,
The old wood is squeaking
A tap is dripping,

It's as though their speaking,

Telling me to sort it out.

When I come down the stairs its all about,

I THINK I'M DOWN AND OUT !

RADIATORS OLD

The old radiator is leaking again,

The old fire timer I'm seeking again.

Getting warmer, eating chicken korma.
Spring is coming its getting warmer.

THE RAIN

It rained all night.

It rains all day in the garden.

It rained on the front and in the Schoolyard.

It rained on the children.

It rained, I went out and was wet through.
It rained on my trousers, it rained on the yard.

It rained on the park.

It rained till dark.

It rained in the evening, it rained all day.
It rained through so I couldn't go out to play.

THE BEAUTIFUL BUTTERFLY

My Sister is a beautiful butterfly,
She ascended from the earth.
She's happy now in heaven,
She was so down to earth.
Florence was a special person,
She was a guiding light,
Sometimes she suffered,
She always did what was right.
I know she's free.
My sister is a butterfly.
She's no longer a caterpillar,
She finally won the fight.
She is a beautiful butterfly,
She's finally taken flight.

To my beautiful sister Florence 1956-2002

Love Anthony.

2001

This is the year 2001, with traffic jams in
the air and violence every where.
In this world of supersonic, people cannot move without atomic.
We wear gas masks all the time let's hope I never forget mine.
Would you believe today I saw a sparrow,
But a man shot it with a bow and arrow.
For that Sparrow the man bought a golden arrow
If I were the governor of this land, I'd cover it up with
soil and sand and "bring back nature to England".

(One of Anthony's earliest Poems written in 1977).

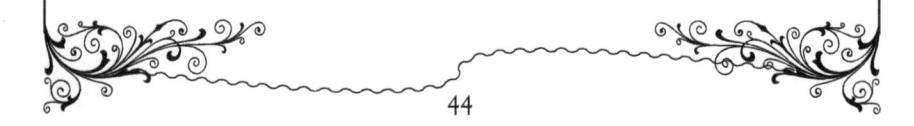

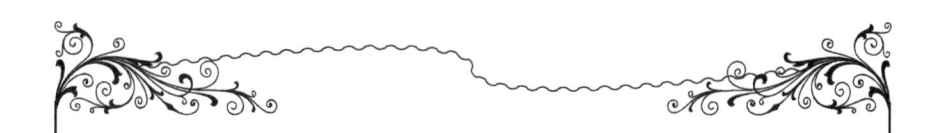

THE SNOB

Why do you hate me?
I'm your friend I call for you.
When so down I made you laugh
Comforted you when you're around.

So why do you hate me?
I'm your friend,
Right to the end.

I saw you staring at me at the bus stop,
Waiting for my every move.
So why do you hate me?

You look down on me in your snobbery.
So why do you hate me?

I'm too fair,
I'm your friend.
You're not a friend, so there!

They wear lovely clothes, fancy dresses.
They try to impress, fancy clothes and fancy dresses,
Fancy frills.

They are the elite, the special ones.
They do matter.

They come from towns.
They're never last, they're never worst.
They drink the fanciest wine, having a good time.

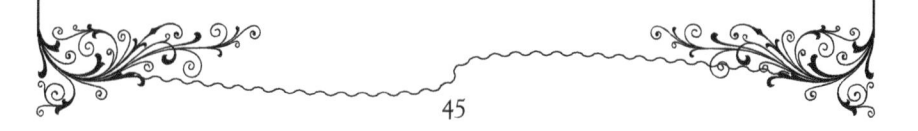

They kid themselves with their fancy worldly goods.
They want to go on a spaceship to the moon.

They're living in a dream,
It's a great scene.
Their worldly ways never pays.

They want to go on a spaceship to the seven seas.
Bare land for you and me.

Their blind with ambitious ways.
The power Games their aim.
They don't forget their worldly ways.

By Anthony Warren Bardsley
August 2008

A WALK THROUGH STOCKPORT

I went for a walk down Stockport
I saw the Mersey Square,
And the Pigeons there all about sung in the air.
I saw the River Mersey, and got back at the market store.
The town shopping centre
I like Stockport Square.
The Post Office old house sounded a bell, and sang aloud.
And I like the River Mersey.
I like Daw Bank, I like Underbank.
I like the shops.
I saw a bus, it was going fast down Stockport Square.
The Bingo Theatre.
I caught a bus to Edgeley, the number eleven.
I saw Edgeley at the County Square,
They scored a goal.
The town Stockport is my favourite town.

TRAMPS NOT THIEVES

This is a story of tramps not thieves.

Who built a house of twigs and leaves.

Instead of lying on the Doss house floor

They hunted like wild Ducks Galore.

(One of Anthony's earliest Poems from the 1970's)

MUM AND DAD AND ME

Mum and Dad and Me went to the January sales
Florence bought a bubble coat, Gerard bought some shoes.
We went
down Andrew Square, up Lancashire Bridge, past St Josephs
down King Street, up Princess Street, down near the market
up Shaw Heath, down to the shopping centre.

Dad, Me, Florence, Gerard and Mum went to the Co-op and bought a scone and a cup of hot chocolate and a meal and went to the market place
Then we went to Marks and Spencers.

Gerard and Me bought some trousers and some jumpers and some summer coats
Then we went down the shops and then caught the 386 back home.

Just walking down Andrew Square, home with Mum and Dad, we had some scones.

Mum and Dad made me and Gerard some crumpets and some milk puddings
Then we sat down and watched TV

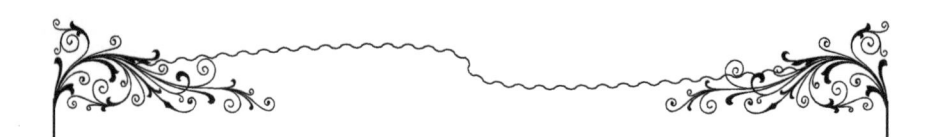

I love my Mum and Dad
They tucked us in at night
and they said
"Goodnight"
We slept all night

I love my parents, they treat us right
We woke up in the morning
everything was alright
They made us see the light
Mum and Dad are alright

They made our future bright
They made us do
what was right
"Night night"
Our family is alright, we saw the light. Mum and Dad are alright

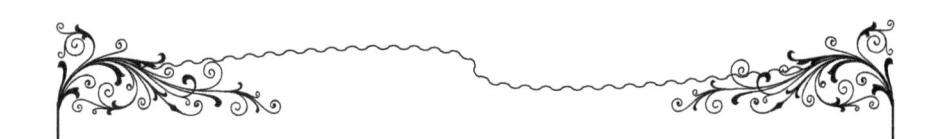

WORLDLY GOODS

Are they going places?
They're going to the pub
I'm watching from my lonely bedroom window
Are they happy in happy worldly world?

The neon light shines brightly on the street
They're buying a meal in a pub and restaurant
Do they know what to do?
Are they pulling through?
Are they settled in little worldly world?

The summer rain is pouring down
Leaving me with a weary frown
Happy in the town, leaving me with a weary frown

STUCK IN MY ROOM

Stuck in my room
Singing that tune
Staring at the moon
I just happen to be
Never to see my fantasy
Never come true
When sat in my room
Never see my fantasy

ALLEY ROAD

I walked down the Alley Road
Down Complimentary Lane
And into the supermarket
I went into a convenience store
I spotted a felt hat with a cane feather frame
And a ribbon rim
And a large collared beam with cotton tape

It fits around my head
With a rim, so soft in the middle
A nice soft head rim
A string rim, fitting well on my head
And a strong black glow
A suede leather frame where my head did go

About a pound. One pound did you say?
It's ten weeks before Christmas
Will keep my head warm from the cold
And snow white
Where the sun did go slow, you know
A week ago it was going slow you know

It was a lovely cane collared hat
My hat it was big
So the sun sheltered me from the rain, with a frame

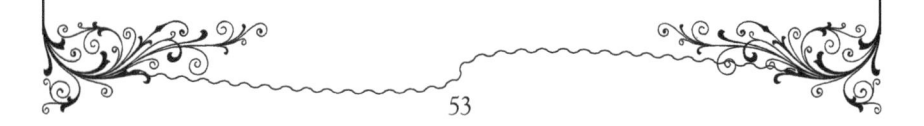

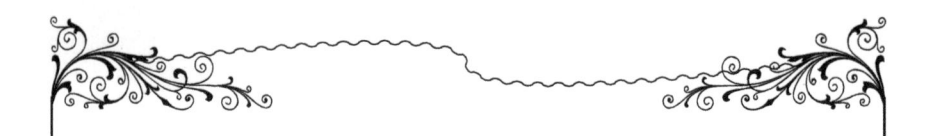

Pitter patter goes the rain
And where my head did fit, heavy showers did fall

I like my hat
It was a lovely hat
So soft in the middle, with a ribbon
I love that hat
I love my hat so; it told me where to go
Told me where to go
I want to come out when the sun comes up

It was a lovely hat

UP ROMILEY

Up through Werneth Low,
up Marsden Road,
down Broughton Road,
down Compstall Road,
up Sandy Lane
up Broughton Road
down Sandy Lane
into Romiley Parks
near Stockport Road - cause I'm going nowhere

Never got it made
Never made much of myself
Never make my name
Not doing well
Never going anywhere

It seems such a shame
I'm just to blame
I'll never make my name.

I see the people are going places
They seem to have it made
I'm such a shame
Cause I can't get it made.

I look through the window
it seems such a shame
I'll never make my name
it seems such a shame
I'll never make my name
Maybe I'm the one to blame
it seems such a shame

SWEET CHILD OF MINE

O sweet child of joy, you have so far to go
Talk of death you never know
Crying in my arms, you gently charm
You are a little child of love
A hope from Heaven, a gift from high above
Gently you sleep, you are so full of love
Full of love, gently sleep, gently sleep

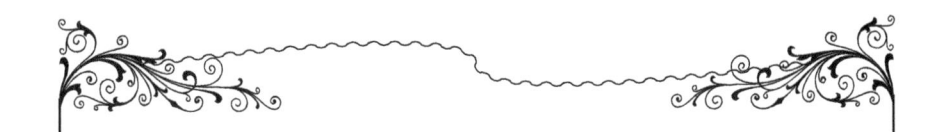

OLD PEOPLE

When I was young, I was dancing in the rain
Singing in the snow
Waving to the day
Where they danced without a care
Wishing for the future

They're getting married
Looking to the future
Hold hand to hand
Playing to the pleasant
Hoping with their plans
Making for their vacation
Where there's fun and laughing
On a journey far away.

Waiting for the springs
But old age wrinkles them
They grow old and grey
Young days gone and youth seems to pass them away
Young days are going away.

HOSPITAL BED

Lying in a hospital bed
waiting the night
and the light
watching for the morning
sleeping with a yawning
feeling withdrawn
remembering being born
waiting till dawn
for a cup of tea
in the morn

Lying in my bed
Feeling that I'm dead
Waiting for my results
With a dread
Waiting for the doctor
To come around
On his rounds

Reading the paper
I want to go to the disinfectant ward

Drinking orange juice and lemonade and eating grapes
Waiting for the lovely nurses bringing an afternoon meal.
Eating rice pudding and egg custard and my favourite kind of drink.

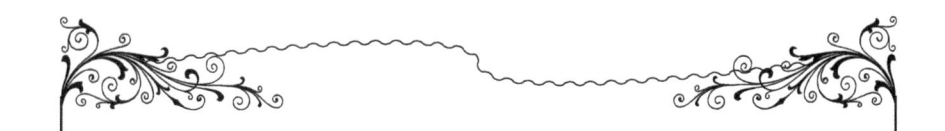

I may be coming home
Wishing to be discharged
Little and Large
Lay in my bed a long time
And lying awake with no sleep
Lying in a heap
Feeling fast asleep
Sliding far away
Watching through my window
Watching people going out for the night
Are they going to the pub and restaurants?
Watching from my room
Are they going places in their little world?

Have they got it made?
Going to the restaurant, the world.

People think they've got it made, going down the road
Going to the arcades, the world.
People think that they've got it made.
They're going ? destination to a land so far away.
They seem to have it made.

STAY-AT-HOME BILL

Stay at home Bill
I get my fill
My name is Stay-at-home Bill
Sat in my room
In the winter gloom
Sat on my own
Near my phone
All alone
In my lonely home
Sat on my face
Such a disgrace
No-one can see
Facing reality
What morality
Facing ferocity
Sat in my room
Singing a weary tune

A CHILD'S VIEW OF JESUS

When I go to Heaven
About a quarter past eleven
When I go to bed, he will tuck me in at night.

He will bring me a cup of tea, and some cornflakes
I will be with my sister and my mother too
You can come too.

In heaven with a smile, a different point of view
I'll know what to do
Let my tears be wiped away, I'll feel ok.

I'll be in Heaven and you can come too
I'll be in Heaven forever with Jesus
He'll make me important
A better place for me and you.

I'LL BE READY

I'll be ready when the white dove flies over the sky
I wonder why, I wonder why
For my time's up, when my time's up
When I'm at my last breath I will go to a better place
I will know, I will know

To a land of peace and harmony
I want to go to paradise and joy for every girl and boy

When my time's up, when God calls me
I go to Heaven, you can come too

Where my peace of mind, peace and harmony
And go to release and peace
Where my tears release into paradise
I will live in style and I will leave this cruel world behind

And my time is up
And find happiness and peace
On the other side

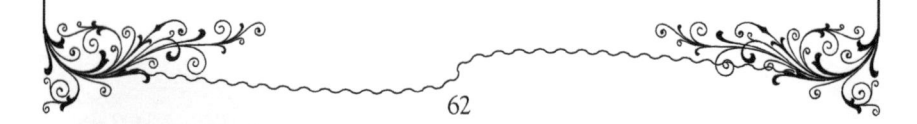

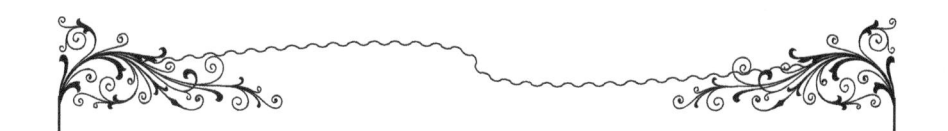

THE COLD'S COMING

Winter's coming!
The cold is coming.

Summer is going!
Nights are long, days are short.

Frosty and icy patches,
Snowy pavements, winter flu's.

Winter clouds, North West breezes,
Winter leaves, winter colds.

Autumn leaves are falling,
Wet and windy, appalling.

Late nights through lack of sleep.
Overwrought, strong coast of west
Winter is the test.

Me I feel the cold
Because I'm getting old.
I'll have to be quite bold,
Because I feel the cold.

Too much sun can blind you,
It can leave you starry-eyed.
And finally you realise
You'll get a big surprise.
Then you'll realise!

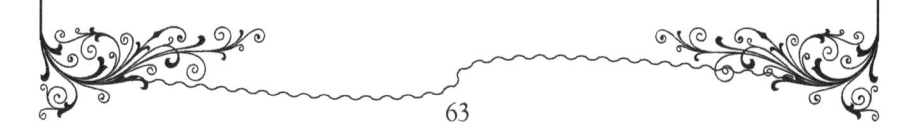

THE GREY WHITE DOVE

The grey white dove, fly high above
Fly high in the sky, with a gentle love

Its never ever dull, always ever grey
Flying high above the sky

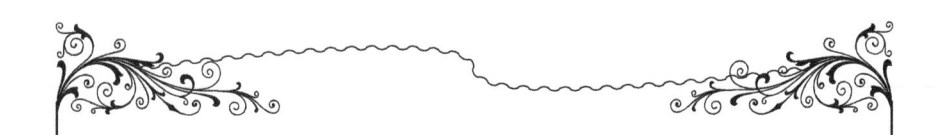

THE WHITE DOVE

He sings in the morning
He sings with joy
He is a grateful thing
He knows I'm in the forest
His happy heart flourished

Happy is the wanderer
He finds his true home
His heart does sing
For the dove does flourish
He is a grateful thing

He rises over the plains
Across the mountain top
He rests on the hillside
Till the morning
His happy heart sings
All day till dark
Then he goes quiet till dawn.

The poet does sleep all night till morning
He hears the dove's coos in the middle of the morning.

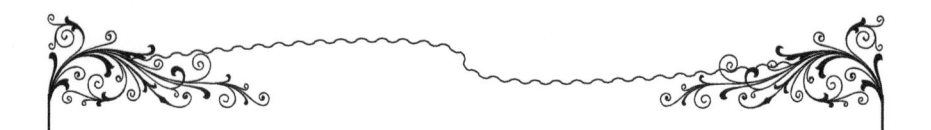

THE LOSING CARD

I run away from what I find in the darkness today
Too much to take in is what I feared
What I saw in front of the door I feared
It seems to me life is so hard and I am on the losing card

I don't know what to do
I have so much trouble to go through
I saw a snarling creature
Staring at it I feared

I had so much time that I spent life scared
and it seems so hard, that life is a losing card

In the end I'll win and I won't give in
I'll put my hope in Jesus!
Maybe life is not a losing card

O YOUNG DESTINATION

O the young
What are your days showing

Are you going?
Maybe a new day is showing
A new destination, home
Is it what it seems
All through your young new dream

To the disco at night
Club at dawn

Are you going to a better place in sound?
Sailing your dream
A better day lies ahead

Does it give you self-esteem?
Walking with the gangs
In the street at night

Are you happy in the street at night?
Does it make you feel alright
In the street tonight?
Are you going to the pub tonight?In the bar?
Not going very far.
Watch your cider in the jar.

ALL THE FUN OF THE FAIR

Come join the ride
then join the arcade
see the ghost train

Put a penny in the laughing clown
see him without a frown
he's never down
he's the laughing clown

We went down the street, saw the arcade in Madam Tussauds, then had fish and chips on the pier

We went on the promenade, bought some candy outside and some rock

Walked to Bispham, St Annes on Sea, Lytham and Cleveleys along the promenade

Went on a tram, saw the lights then went back to the arcade

Went on a ride, the rollercoaster, then went to the beach, bought ice-cream and went on a donkey too for a ride

then walked the seaside.

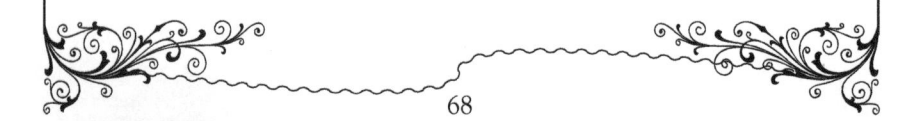

THE GREEN GRASS

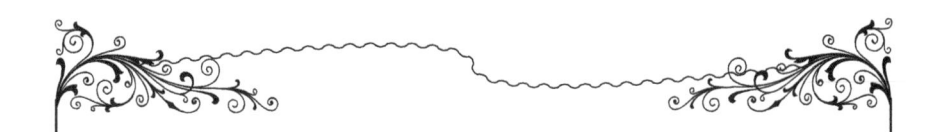

The green grass of Tangshutt fields
The stream of soggy ground
The flowing wind blew over the wind blown chair
The Frog jumping in the stream
The flowing wind in the sky over the grass fields
The Bards are singing angelic songs
Along the grass was growing on.

To Hyde Bank Farm pedestrians walking their dogs
The Bats in their wooden box
They eat wild insects in delight
In the middle of the night
Flapping around the field around the river flows
Through the the river outside the stream
The sun was shining then in the month of May
The pathway on the way was not in decay
On the pathway the dark winter nights
In the middle of the day
Over the hills and faraway
On the day the sunshine over the sunbeam
The battered wind over the park
In the middle of the dark
Feeling ok near the grass on a spring day
On a summers day feeling ok
On the month of May feeling ok
On a summers day
Feeling ok today
I am ok on a summer's day!

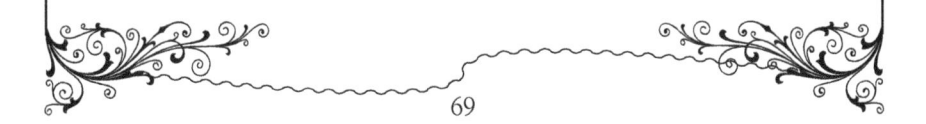

HATRED

Why don't people like me?
They never raise a smile
They look at me like I'm vile.

I'm a kind hearted soul
Why don't people like me?
I got low self esteem

There's something special about me
I'm a lovely person

I worry if I will end up like Jesus, persecuted on the cross
I'll die a horrible death
And they seem to have it in for me

I worry they're jealous of me
Because I'm different
I have a certain style
They never wear a smile

I think I'm a nice person
They look at me as though I'm vile
They never raise a smile

They look at me like I'm an irritation
They look at me because I'm vile
Why don't people like me?
Because I have self denial

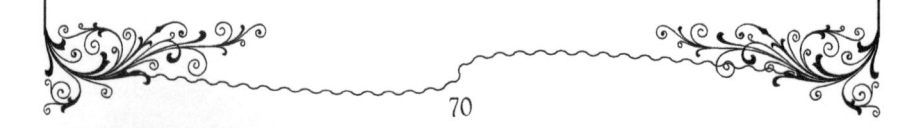

STARING THROUGH MY ROOM

Staring through my room
Through my winter gloom
I watch the children play
Day by day by day

Staring through my room
Winter feels so cold
for I am getting old
Staring through my room

I watch the winter gloom
Staring through my room
Because I am disabled
I hang about, never go out

I am disabled

THE QUEEN BEE

The Queen of the Isle
Has a certain smile and sense of style
With an open hand and an open heart
She's so smart

A loving soul and a gracious heart and style
A loving heart and a certain style, a loving smile

The Queen of the Isle, a certain smile
And a loving soul, a loving heart
And a gracious style
And a loving smile
With a certain style

The Queen of the Isle
A determined soul, with a goal
And a loving smile
With a certain style
And a loving certain smile

The Queen of the Isle

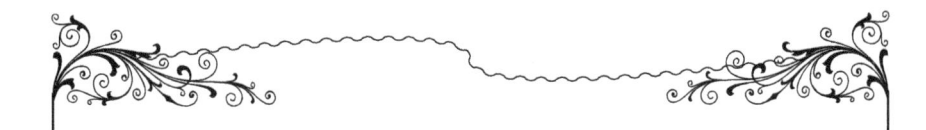

WINTER CHILLS

Snow falling all around
On soggy, frosty ground

Making icy patches all around
Morning mist and frosty ground

Falling on snow and all around
Making darkness, foggy all around

March westwinds, right through
April, May, June, July and August
Bringing out lambs and brighter too

September, October, November gales
Making it cold all around
January, February too, going cold all around
Shaking colder chills all around

Chasing colder chills
Chasing away Winter ills

Pitter, patter goes the rain
Its driving me insane
I'd love to see the Summer again
Driving away the rain
I'd love to see the Summer again
Pitter, patter goes the rain
I'd love to see the Summer again

SUMMER BRINGS LIGHTNING

Now that summer is here
My heart begins to fear

The lightening is here
And the clamminess is here

Lying in my bed I fear
Waiting for a flash to appear
When a flash is near

The stormy weather is here
The lightening shone in the air
The clamminess is here

There's clamminess in the air
There's something in the air because summer is here

Because summer is finally here the clocks go forward
Because summer is here

Take care, summer is here
There's a lightening flash nearby
A thunder in the sky

The clamminess is here
A lightening flash in the sky
The clamminess is near

So summer is here, take care
Take care, take care
Summer is finally here!

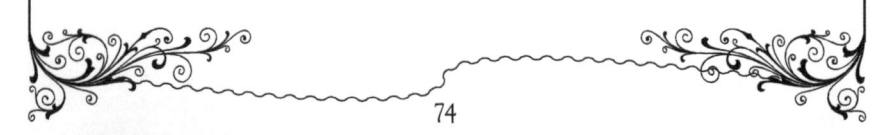

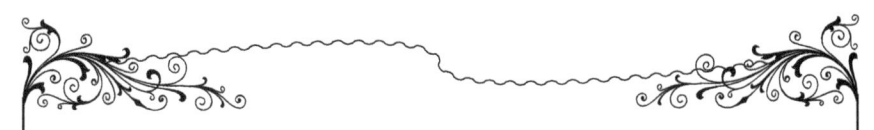

SUNLIGHT

It was early evening
Early in July, about nine o clock.
The street lamplight reflected a shining light
From the sunlight in the street

The sunlight shone it's reflection on the window frame
Like a painting
A picture of a perfect light, shining
Evening sunlight as a reflection on my window

I remember
On the window pane, I remember Newbridge Lane

There were some large steps reaching high to Heaven's sky
Closer than heaven at the top
I tried to climb the steps to the top at Newbridge Lane

I was petrified
My leg went wobbly in the middle of the steps
I fell at the middle step and
People were watching me, they thought I was hurt

I have a terrible paranoia
I thought people didn't care about me
But they phoned for an ambulance
And an ambulance came for me
I had minor bruises and they sent me home

On the way back I heard doves, making a cooing sound
It made me think of peace.
Then did my fears release

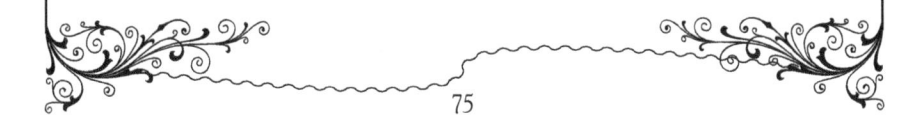

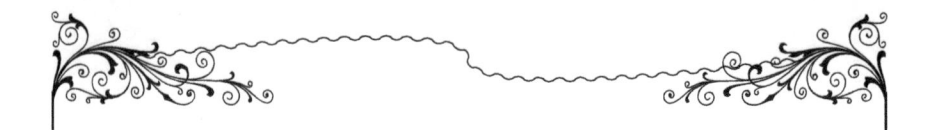

I was welcomed home by my little brother
He made me a cup of tea. I was happy. I went to bed

Next morning, the sunlight shone through the window's reflection again
I felt happy

I saw a reflection through the window again
I listened

I heard the doves making a cooing sound again
A homely song

I felt happy again because I knew people cared about me

My paranoia wasn't so real, I was glad
I was a lovely lad, I wasn't bad

I was a lovely lad
I had thought that my paranoia was real, I realise it wasn't true
I'm happy now because I know I'm a lovely lad
I'm not so sad, as I'm not so bad
Cause I'm not so sad cause I'm not so bad cause I'm a lovely lad cause I'm not so bad

A lovely lad, I'm glad
Cause people care about me

I am glad
A happy lad
I'm a lovely lad
And I'm glad, cause
I'm a lovely lad

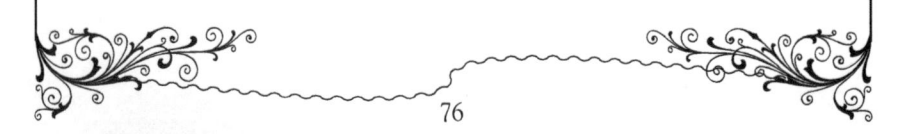

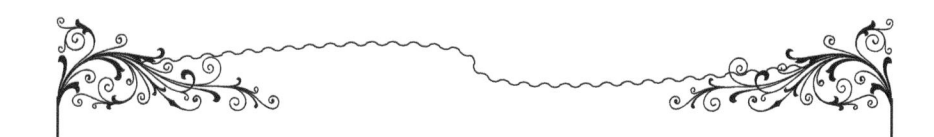

EARTH AND STARS

I am old like the sand

Wisdom is my friend

Knowledge is my refuge

Sunshine is my smile

Darkness is my enemy

Laughter is my food

Long is the road to the end

Of time poetry is my rhyme

Tomorrow is my time

Heaven is my smile

Death is the end

Wisdom is my friend

Heaven is the end

Eternity is the beginning

Happiness is the end

HAVING NOT AND HAVE NOTHINGS

I'm not very fit,
I'm getting on a bit.

Slowing down,
Wearing a frown.

Young days gone,
Wrinkles shone.

Aged so much,
Out of touch.

Over the hill.
Better days seen,
Low esteem.

Less active, giving up,
Tummy up.

A Dinosaur getting old,
Any road.

Too old to carry on, any road,
Getting old.

By Anthony Warren Bardsley

August 2009

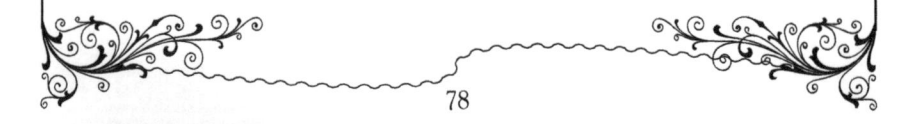

I SAW A SHOOTING STAR

Then I looked in the sky, I saw a great blue star
Maybe I will never get that far.
I can see a shooting star.

May be I'm nothing special at all, may be you are what you are.
I can see a shooting star.

May be I know nothing at all.
Today I saw a shooting star,
May be I couldn't get that far.
If I could see a shooting star!

By Anthony Warren Bardsley

I SAW THAT PLANE

Where does the plane go?

Look in the sky

Home and dry

Look up so high

I try to look up.

So high the plane go slow

Up and down the wind does blow.

Where does that plane go?

Quck slow, quick slow

Where does that plane go?

I don't know

Quick slow, quick slow,

Quick the engine go.

Anthony Warren Bardsley.

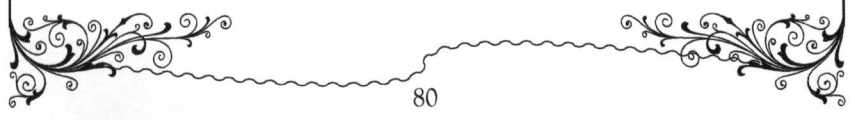

IN THE CARE HOME

In the care home suburban flat
Big house disabled toilet
A wheel chair ramp
Spastic people watching TV.

All day long retarded spastics
In bed watching TV,
Walking up the staircase
The staircase waiting for their drugs.

Tablets from the tablet cabinet box,
Giving out medicine in another cabinet box
Handing out to patients in Tupperware beaker,
Sometimes a Tupperware cup.

Got no girlfriend causing depression.
Handicapped residents, big butch nurses
Not allowing any pity,
Young student nurses looking rather pretty.

Roxanne's from Soho town, worked in a sauna house.
Liked by all men,
I wonder if I will see her again,
Our Roxanne.

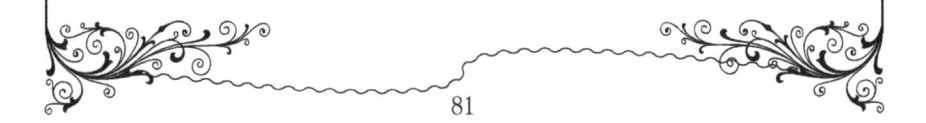

Roxanne's a lovely girl
She makes the men feel good,
She makes them feel happy,
She comes from Soho Town.

She's there in the middle of the city,
She has a certain style,
She wears that certain smile
She always makes us smile.

Roxanne is a lovely girl I wonder if I will see her again,
Maybe tomorrow, maybe today,
Maybe next month,
Maybe in a while.

LITTLE CHILDHOOD JOE

Oh my darling little Joe.
You have so far to go.
Many adventures to explore,
"South Sea Island on a Pirate Ship",
Across the seven seas.
Climbing up trees.

Braving the cold,
Playing warriors so bold.

Because I'm a poet getting old.

It's about your childhood story tiny little Joe.
You have so far to go,
Because you're a child so courageous and bold.
Going to the Football Match,
Scoring a goal,
Watching action at Bower Fold.

Going to Stockport County my favourite side,
Playing at Bower Fold your story told.

You're a child you have far to go.
Because your best.

I like my adventure in my tender years.

Live for today,
Or some horrible beggar will take it away.
Take away your tender years.

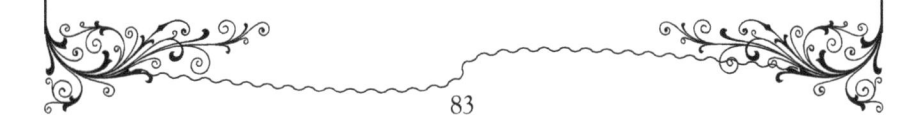

Because I'm supposed to be wise.
But I'm still a little child.

When you can, because you're a little man,
Don't throw it all away.

Live for today, do the best you can,
Because be wise, because I'm still a little child.
I'm still a little child,
I'm still a little man.

Little Childhood Joe, I suddenly don't feel very well.

My older sister phoned the ambulance today,
Because my body and mind began to swell.

I'm on a casualty ward
When my fears began.

You see I cannot be with you in your youthful years.

I don't want to lose my grip on life.
I'll wait for the Surgeons Knife.

So Darling little Joe, don't lose your grip,
Do the best you can.

Don't lose your plan,
Because you're a little man.

By Anthony Warren Bardsley

February 2014.

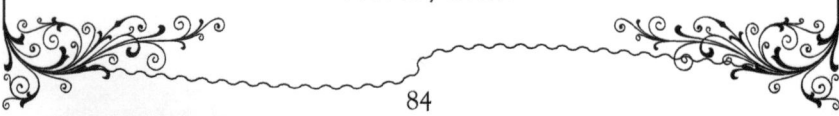

MY MOTHER CARED FOR ME

Mother said she loved me, before she passed away
My parents were proud of me.
Before they passed away I knew my parents loved me.
Before they passed away, she showed it in her heart.
I wasn't the Black Sheep of the family,
Because my parents loved me I saw it in their eyes.
They adored me.

My parents were very good to me.
They were proud of my great poetical talent,
I impressed them.
My parents did so much for me.
I wasn't the black sheep of the family.
My parents loved me.
They loved me so I saw their love, I loved them.

I realised they loved me,
I wasn't the black sheep of the family.
My parents were proud of me,
I wasn't their black sheep of the family
They were proud of me,
They took me on holidays,
Like Skegness, Lytham St Anne's, Bispham, Prestatyn,
Talacare Beach, Tenby, Rome and Lourdes, Colwyn Bay
And also a sunny day in Scarborough fair they say.

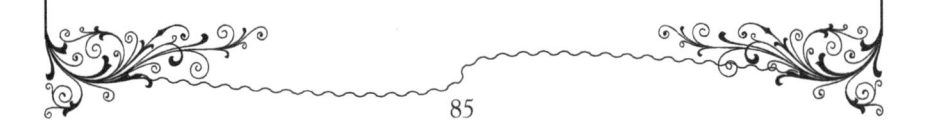

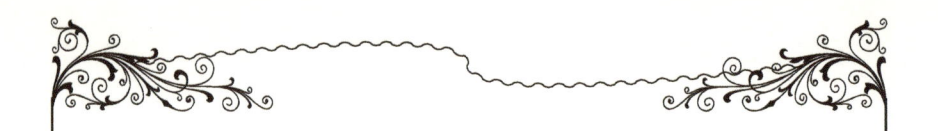

After my mother passed away,
My father took me to Ireland, he took me to Abbeyfeale.
I remember when I was a child,
My parents bought me a large bag of fish and chips in
Scarborough, I knew I was loved.

Now my parents and sister have passed away.
They left me, they left me standing on my own,
They have gone to paradise.
I knew then I wasn't the black sheep of the family.
I knew I was loved, because I was loved,
Because they loved me.

THE MOUNTAIN OF HEAVEN

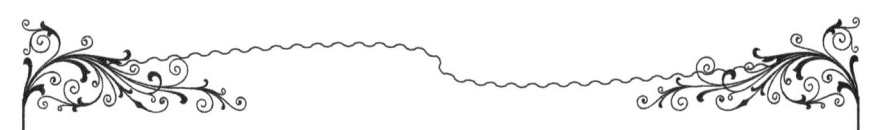

The mountain of Heaven,
Kinder Scout near Smithy Green Road
Kinder View on a Bumpity Icy
Horses in the farm in the Rocky Road
Muddy Pavement, one Collie dog.
There's one above the lane
At Kitty Cottage.

Lovely old field lane with Sheep dipping in the mud,
Cattle in the field chewing the cud.
Blue Hazy sky, lovely view
The day I wandered there.
Seagulls moving from in land
Escaping the clammy weather.
I wonder if it's a sign of snowy weather.

January Frost, South Atlantic rain
Moving from the South Atlantic.
Bringing milder weather,
Escaping from the outside watching TV.
I wonder if there's a Horror Movie on today.
I loved Kitty Cottage,
I stayed there for a week.

Today I went to Marple Bridge in a café.
They served tea and crumpets on special days,
Watching Comedy of Errors on TV today.
Kinder View from the city waiting,
Watching television all day.
Never going outside, not getting any exercise.
But I felt so good inside; I wonder if I will sleep tonight.

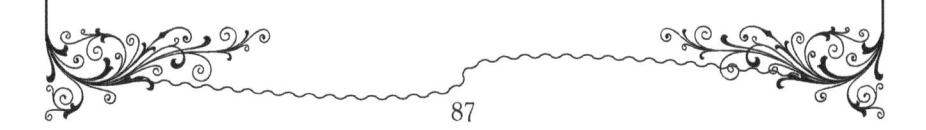

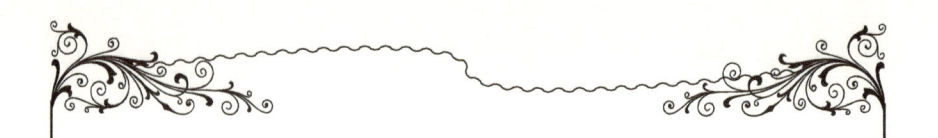

Sat on a sofa cushion sitting in a lovely lounge,
I loved the lovely view from the Cottage outside.
The Kitty Cottage outside, it was a lovely view.
Walking in the countryside it was a lovely view,
Outside Kitty Cottage a lovely distant view.
Silk Satin sheets, a lovely cushioned armchair,
Lovely Satin Curtains.

The shower and bath were lovely,
And a lovely brown vinyl floor.
I now wonder if I will sleep tonight.
Now that I am home,
Far away from lovely Kitty Cottage,
And the Collie in the lane.
Now missing that lovely Kinder View.

ANTHONY'S QUOTATIONS

"Perfection is a weakness"

"A wise old fool"

"The rich are poor"

"The poor are rich"

"The man with everything has nothing"

"The man with nothing has everything"

Lightning Source UK Ltd.
Milton Keynes UK
UKHW011526160921
390686UK00001B/325